Heads Up!

D0095682

How To Use This Book

There are lots of extras in this book aimed at helping you with research projects.

BRAIN JAM

Brain Jams offer activities to get you thinking creatively and give you a chance to hone your skills.

★ PROJECT JUMP START

Project Jump Starts provide that sometimes necessary extra push to get you going on your own research project.

TIP FILE

Tip Files offer up all sorts of helpful suggestions and hints on getting the project done.

RESOURCES   RESOURCES

One of these icons will lead you to more information.

ORDINARY   EXTRAORDINARY

Throughout the book, you will see the ordinary and the extraordinary side by side. With revisions and some thought, these comparisons show you what you can accomplish.

Photographs © 2006: Phyllis Reynolds Naylor/Rex Naylor: 33; Jason Stemple: 38; Corbis Images: 118.

Cover design: Marie O'Neill
Series design: Simon Says Design and Marie O'Neill
Art production: The Design Lab
Cover and interior illustrations by Kevin Pope

Library of Congress Cataloging-in-Publication Data

Orr, Tamra B.
  Extraordinary research projects / by Tamra B. Orr.
    p. cm. — (F.W. prep)
  Includes bibliographical references and index.
  ISBN 0-531-16762-3 (lib. bdg.)   0-531-13907-7 (pbk.)
  1. Report writing—Handbooks, manuals, etc. 2. Research—Handbooks, manuals, etc.
I. Title. II. Series.
  LB1047.3.O77 2006
    371.3'028'1—dc22   2005021566

EXTRAORDINARY
Research Projects

by Tamra B. Orr

Franklin Watts®

A Division of Scholastic Inc.
New York • Toronto • London • Auckland • Sydney
Mexico City • New Delhi • Hong Kong
Danbury, Connecticut

EXTRAORDINARY RESEARCH PROJECTS

HOW-TO MINI-GUIDES

THE BACK MATTER

ASSIGNMENT:

Up until now, life has gone pretty well.
You are keeping up in most of your classes,
you are finally getting the hang of conjugating
French verbs, and you managed to get
through your math test without passing out
from stress. But now, everything is different.
Your teacher spoke those dreaded words—
"research project." Despair ripples through the
room and slams right into you.

Believe it or not, these projects are not
assigned just to torture you. Essays are part
of the plan your state has for your education.
Each state has its own educational curriculum
plan for you and other students in your states.
These plans are called educational standards.
From **New York** to **Utah,** from **Illinois** to
Louisiana, the standards call for students to
tackle a variety of research projects. In New
York, for instance, students in grades nine
through twelve are expected to write and
present research reports on a variety of topics
in all subject areas. Educators in Louisiana
want students to be able to identify topics
and gather and evaluate information from
a variety of sources.

Research Project

All over the country, other students just like you are rolling up their sleeves and tackling the demanding research project. They are searching for ideas, doing research, taking notes, managing their time, and writing draft after draft. If everyone else is doing it, how in the world are you supposed to make yours unique and interesting? In other words, how do you make yours **EXTRAORDINARY**?

The key to making your research project—or anything else you might be doing for school—stand out from the crowd is knowing what you are expected to do and then going way past that. These projects are not only a chance to impress your teacher and get a good grade; they are a chance for you to learn important writing and organization skills that you will use many times in the future.

Primary sources are pouring in on the East Coast and the Gulf Coast is awash in science fair project papers.

7

Check Out Your State's Standards!

If you want a chance to peek into your future, take a look at your state's standards for your grade and the grades yet to come. You can find them at the Developing Educational Standards Web site: **http://www.edstandards.org/Standards.html**

On this site, you can find links to the educational departments of every state in the country. If you'd like an even more thorough peek at educational standards, you can find lots of information at the site of the National Council of Teachers of English, **http://www.ncte.org.**

By researching and writing extraordinary research projects, you are demonstrating a number of key skills mentioned in the standards:

- Completing an extraordinary research project shows that you are able to read a wide range of print and nonprint texts to build an understanding of sources and to acquire new information.

- The organizational tools you use while writing an extraordinary research project demonstrates your knowledge of writing strategies and the writing process.

- An extraordinary research project involves conducting research, posing questions, and examining the issues surrounding a topic.

- To create an extraordinary research project, you must gather and analyze information from a variety of resources, including technological ones.

- In writing an extraordinary research project, you must be able to use spoken, written, and visual language to accomplish the purposes of learning and exchanging information.

Heads Up!

So Here's the Scoop

When teachers grade your research project, they look carefully at several factors to determine your grade. Although this information can change from class to class and teacher to teacher, these are the general guidelines for how your research project will be graded:

Focus: Did you stay on topic or stray from your main points? Was your focus too broad, too narrow, or just right?

Research: Were the facts relevant and timely? Did they support the thesis statement?

Organization: Did the project flow from one fact to another? Did it transition easily from your words to the words of others?

Authenticity: Did you make sure to give credit to your sources? Did you make sure not to take the credit yourself? Did your quotes and summaries support your own original ideas?

Documentation: Did you use the proper type of footnoting or other documentation?

G.U.M. (aka Grammar, Usage, and Mechanics): Did you remember to check your punctuation, spelling, and grammar? Was your vocabulary varied and lively?

What's a Research Project Anyway?

If you break down the word **research,** you can see that it means to "search again." When you work on a research project, you:

- **Look up information, facts, and ideas that have already been stated, discovered, or published.**

- **Take that wide variety of information and put it together in a new way.**

- **Add your own perspective and opinions.**

But remember, if you only get your information from one place, or if you only depend on your own knowledge, your project will fail.

Putting together a research project in school is important. That should be clear from the time and attention your teachers give to it. Often this project takes up weeks of class time and may count for a great portion of your overall class grade. Completing a research project is also good practice for college, where this type of writing may be required much more frequently.

Whatever profession you may end up pursuing, being able to study a subject deeply, interpret information from multiple resources, and then put it all together in an organized fashion will help you.

Even when your formal education is behind you, you are likely to find yourself in a job that requires some of these very same writing and organizational skills. Your boss may ask you to conduct a survey, do an interview, and read some abstracts, and then put together a business plan or a memo or a report. You may be asked to go online and download pertinent articles, summarize them, and then provide your opinions on the topic. The skills you learn now are the ones that will help you sail right through those kinds of assignments.

Types of Research Projects

Research projects have the same basic foundation but may go in slightly different directions, depending on the class in which they are assigned. In this book, you will learn the basics and then take a special look at:

English Class Research Projects

Your English teacher will almost certainly assign you a research project. This is nearly always an in-depth paper that can range from three to more than a dozen pages.

Science Class Research Projects

You may find yourself enrolled in this year's science fair and need a project for it. Like a paper, this will require research and organization, but it will also require you to incorporate visuals.

History/Social Studies Research Projects

These classes may have you focus on a moment in history or a global issue and put the information into a paper, a display, or a combination of both.

Heads Up!

So What's a Research Project?

A research project is:

- an in-depth look at a topic;

- a compilation of facts and information from a variety of resources;

- something that requires investigation and detailed note taking.

Most research projects consist of:

- an idea stated in a thesis statement;

- supporting evidence such as quotes, summaries, and paraphrases;

- special documentation.

Documentation

Format

Thesis statement

length

Sources

MI

APA

On

Revise

Conclusion

14

HUNT AND GATHER

Finding Your Idea

Finding Your Idea

In a few weeks, you are going to have to turn in a research project for your class. There is no escaping it, unless you arrange to leave the country—and if you do, rest assured that any school you end up at will require them, too!

There are twelve basic steps involved in completing a research project, so this is not something you can put off until the weekend before it is due. The more time you have to complete it, the better. Don't panic, either. Take one step at a time—break it down into smaller bits so it does not seem so overwhelming.

Heads Up!

The Twelve-Step Program for Research Projects

1. Select an idea.

2. Narrow down the idea and get the right spin on it.

3. Develop a thesis statement.

4. Do your research and take notes.

5. Make an outline.

6. Write the first draft.

7. Focus on the introduction.

8. Create a strong conclusion.

9. Integrate resources and quotes in the body.

10. Revise, revise, revise.

11. Pull together the front and back matter.

12. Print and submit.

Step one is simple: finding and perfecting the idea.

Every single thing that has ever been invented, painted, sculpted, or written originally began as someone's idea. This is equally true of your research project. Your teacher may have made this part a lot easier for you by assigning you a topic. If you get to choose your own idea, you can choose one that you like. As Jerry Spinelli, author of **Maniac Magee** and many other best-selling young adult novels, says, "The golden rule of writing is to write what you care about. If you care about the topic, you'll do your best writing, and then you stand the best chance of really touching a reader in some way."

Ideas are everywhere and virtually limitless, so if you are feeling completely stumped and your mind is blank, don't worry. This chapter will help you figure out not only where to look for one, but also how to make sure it is just right.

TIP FILE

To check to see if you really understand the specifications for the assignment, see if you can repeat them to a classmate or your parents by heart. Did you remember all of the guidelines without looking? If you did, that's great. If not, read it over again and see what you missed.

Begin at the beginning: look at the assignment.

This is the time to really pay attention. Make sure to carefully follow the directions your teacher provides. This information is absolutely essential to your project's success. The teacher's directions should contain all of the main elements of the assignment. If you miss one, it can spell catastrophe. For example, if the directions call for a paper that is supposed to be 5,000 words long and you write 2,000, you're sunk. Even if those 2,000 words are wonderfully written without a single mistake, you are still sunk.

5,000 words?
I thought it
was 500!

You're missing
a zero!
5,000 — not 4,999
but 5,000 . . .

Assignment Checklist

Although your teacher may not hand you your research project idea on a golden platter, there are a number of details that will be provided. Pay attention to the following:

Length: How long should it be? Usually your teacher will explain that in one of two ways: word count or page count. It may need to be 5,000 words or between five and seven pages.

Number and type of sources: How many resources does your teacher want you to use? How many different types? Are there certain dates you have to stick to?

Form of documentation: Does your teacher want endnotes? Footnotes? Neither? Which style manual are you expected to use?

Extra material: Are you supposed to include a bibliography? A title page? A notes page? Visuals? Does the teacher specify any other important info?

Format: Is your paper to be double-spaced? Typed? What font style and size? In a folder?

Due date: When does it have to be done and turned in?

If you do not have these details, ask for them. You can bet if you are wondering, so are your classmates. Ask questions now rather than have to change things later. It's much easier!

When you start looking for an idea, start with your own interests. What intrigues you? What would you like to know more about? What inspires you to look further and deeper? When you were sitting in class studying a certain topic, what got your attention? Did something stand out and inspire you to learn more about it? These are the best places to start when searching for your idea.

"To solve a problem or to reach a goal, you don't need to know all the answers in advance. But you must have a clear idea of the problem or the goal you want to reach."

—W. Clement Stone
(1902–2002)

It's Time for a Brainstorm

Just as with other types of writing, one of the best ways to start the idea process is by brainstorming or freewriting. You can do it in class, with a classmate, with a friend, or by yourself. Focus on what you have been learning about in class and what the teacher wants you to write about—then start writing down thoughts, words, and phrases as they come to you. Don't give much thought to grammar, spelling, or punctuation. Just let the ideas flow from your mind to either a piece of paper or a computer screen. Ask yourself what you already know about the subject and see where that leads you.

Once you have some ideas written down, it's time to pick out the best ones. Cross off the ideas that you know would not work. (A research project on why *Buffy the Vampire Slayer* should be put back on television is most likely not a great choice!) Go over the ones you have left. Pick your five favorites and analyze each one. Which one works best for this type of project? Let's find out.

Ask yourself the following questions about each of your favorite ideas and see what you come up with:

1 Are there entire books on this topic? (Too broad.)

2 Is it hard to think of more than two points to support it? (Too limited.)

3 Is it complicated and hard to understand? (Too technical.)

4 Does it make people get into heated discussions? Could be good—but be prepared for controversy!

5 Is it an idea that you see almost everywhere? (Too common.)

6 Is it a boring idea? (Then it's going to be a boring paper.)

7 Are other people going to be interested in this topic? (Hopefully.)

8 Does the idea fit with what your teacher had in mind? (It had better!)

"Selecting the right topic often determines the success of the paper."

—*Webster's New World Student Writing Handbook*

And the Search Goes On . . .

While your imagination is one of the best places to find ideas, it is not the only one. Here is a list of other places you should check out:

Look through your class textbook. Scan through it for topics you have already covered, as well as those still to come. Which one sparks an interest in you?

Look through your class notes. Glance through some of the notes and handouts you have from class. Are there any places you starred or highlighted because you wanted to know more?

Talk to your teacher. See if your teacher has some resources to recommend or even a list of ideas that have been used in the past, to spur your own original ideas or spin-offs.

Browse the newsstand. Check out the headlines on newspapers and the cover stories of magazines. Find anything interesting?

Watch or listen to news programs. You can hear different viewpoints on current events. Do any of them get you thinking?

Check out the bestseller lists and the new title shelves at the library. While you're at the library, talk to the librarians. You'll probably be surprised how many suggestions they have for you.

Talk to other students. Ask around to see what other students have done their research projects on in the past.

Talk to your family. Almost everyone (even parents!) has had to do a research project at one time or another, so ask your mom, dad, or siblings for their thoughts.

Look through different kinds of media. Look at newspapers, magazines, and television shows for ideas. Inspiration might be found in anything from a commercial to an obituary.

Scan the library shelves. Sometimes book titles can lead you to a topic you hadn't thought about before.

Pay attention! Read, look, listen, and watch what's happening around you. The perfect idea might be right under your nose!

Finding the Right Spin

Let's take a look at how you can home in on the perfect idea with just a little tweaking.

Let's say you are supposed to write a research paper for social studies class on any foreign country that intrigues you. After brainstorming, you finally narrow your list down to **Slovenia**. Your ancestors came from there, so you would like to know more about it. It is pretty clear, however, that one simple research project cannot possibly cover an entire country, so you will need to narrow it down. Maybe you could do something about the **people** there. That's a step in the right direction. Because you are interested in **sports**, you could focus on what sports are popular in Slovenia. That's another step. When you discover that one of the best **ski jumps** in the world is in a town in Slovenia called **Planica**, you've got your idea!

Look at how you narrowed down your idea from too broad to just right:

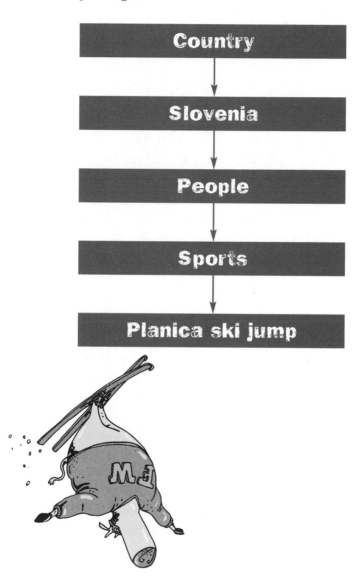

Country

↓

Slovenia

↓

People

↓

Sports

↓

Planica ski jump

"When I'm looking for an idea, I will do anything—clean the closet, mow the lawn, work in the garden."

—Kevin Henkes, author of *Chrysanthemum*

How about if you have to write a research paper for English class on some aspect of your favorite poet? Once again, you are starting with a broad topic— poets—and have to narrow it down from there. So you brainstorm some names and then pick the one you like the best.

If you chose Edward Lear, for example, you would be one step closer. Entire books have been written about this man's life, however, so what should you focus on? How about one of his poems? Depending on the length of the paper you must write, a single poem might be a bit too narrow. Instead, how about focusing on the use of nonsense in his verse? Perhaps you could do a research project on his use of invented words and nonsensical situations. For example, take a look at these lines from his poem "The Dong with a Luminous Nose."

> *"Far and few, far and few,*
> *Are the lands where the Jumblies live;*
> *Their heads are green, and their hands are blue,*
> *And they went to sea in a Sieve."*

Here is what you did with this topic:

Famous poet

↓

Edward Lear

↓

**Nonsense poems/
invented words**

Maybe you have been asked to do a research project in science class. You are expected to back up your words with experiments and visual displays. Your teacher wants something that shows how pollution affects our daily lives. Pollution is a huge topic, ranging from air to water to noise. So first, narrow it down to the one type of pollution you find most interesting. Let's say you pick water pollution. Just writing about the world's levels of water pollution is not only too big but would not fulfill all of the teacher's requirements for experiments. Keep digging. How about a project on how detergents can affect plant growth? Or a project on how much contamination can be found in local ponds? In other words, you took your topic and narrowed it to:

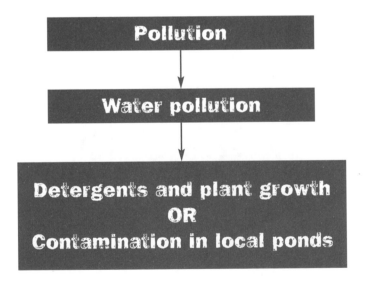

Pollution

Water pollution

Detergents and plant growth
OR
Contamination in local ponds

HIT THE BOOKS

Here are some books that can help
you out in the search for an idea:

*10,000 Ideas for Term Papers, Projects, Reports and
Speeches: Intriguing, Original Research Topics for Every
Student's Needs* by Kathryn Lamm
(Arco Publishing, 1998)

*1001 Ideas for English Papers: Term Papers, Projects,
Reports and Speeches* by Walter James Miller
(Prentice Hall, 1994)

"The best way to have a good idea
is to have a lot of ideas."

—Linus Pauling (1901–1994)

TIP FILE

Keep a pen and a notebook next to your bed. If inspiration happens to hit you as you are drifting off, waking in the middle of the night, or getting up, you will have a way to write down your idea before it is lost.

"Once I have the idea for a story, I start collecting all kinds of helpful information and storing it in three-ring notebooks. . . . I save everything that will help— maps, articles, hand-jotted notes, bits of dialogue from conversations that I overhear."

—Phyllis Reynolds Naylor, author of *Shiloh*

Remember that list of twelve steps at the beginning of the chapter? Well, after finding your idea and narrowing it down, you have only ten steps left. Doesn't time fly when you're having this much fun?

PROJECT JUMP START

★ **Room scan.** Still stuck for an idea? Try this. Stand in the middle of a room such as your bedroom, living room, kitchen, or classroom. Look around and think about what you see. What ideas are within a few feet of you? For example, if you are in the kitchen, how about a history project on the development of appliances? A social studies report on food trends in the United States? Is there a pile of magazines in the room? How about an English project on differences in reading tastes within families?

★ **Call in a favor.** Try sharing the burden. Ask your parents, siblings, or friends to come up with some ideas. Maybe one of their ideas is the perfect topic for your paper. Or maybe listening to their thoughts will set off a brainstorm of your own!

BRAIN JAM:
Turn the Idea Upside Down

One way to make your research project extraordinary is to look at the topic from a new angle. If you are writing about something most people think is wrong, try writing it from the perspective that it is right. If you are writing about a topic that is important to young people, try writing it from the angle of someone who is sixty-five or older. Play the "what-if" game with your idea. What if the South had won the Civil War? What if Hitler had died before he came to power? What if Bram Stoker and Mary Shelley had met and written a book together? What if Earth suddenly stopped spinning?

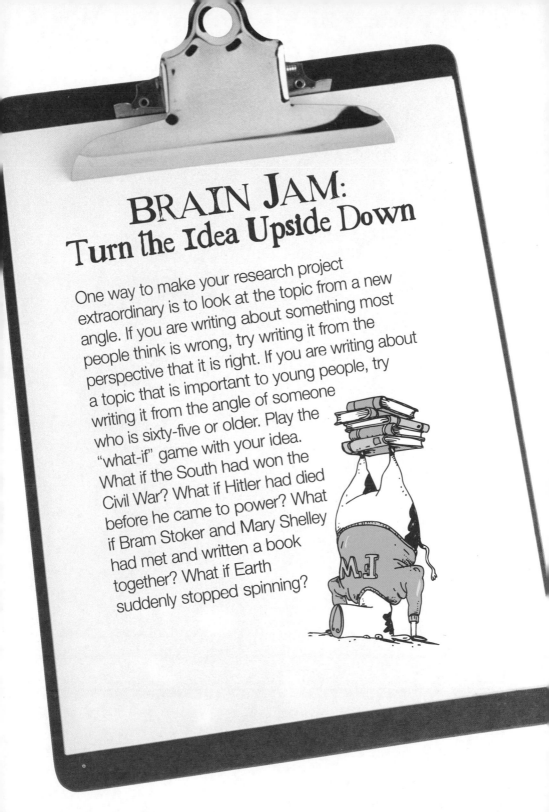

Resources

Internet

Copyright date

Journals

Web site

Li

Museum

Experts

We

Resources

THE VISION

There's a Reason This Is Called a Research Project!

There's a Reason This Is Called a Research Project!

It may seem like a lot of what you are doing to prepare for this project is the same as writing the usual essay or report. You are right, but that is all about to change. In this chapter, you will see exactly why these projects got their name. No matter the topic or the class, these projects center around one thing: **research**. In fact, when it comes to time management, you need to know that most of your time should be spent on the research aspect of your project. It takes far longer than the writing process. So, let's talk about where to find information, how to evaluate it, how to keep track of it, and how to use it wisely.

"Ideas are the cheapest part of the writing. They are free. The hard part is what you do with the ideas you've gathered."

—Jane Yolen, author of *Owl Moon*

Making a Statement

Before you step off the diving board and plunge into the world of research, however, you need to have a direction in which to head. Guidance will come from your thesis statement. Simply put, a *thesis statement* tells the main idea of your project, its purpose, and how you will get there. It should be clear, interesting, and specific. A confusing or boring thesis statement will lead to a confusing or boring paper.

Ask a question. When you sit down to write your thesis statement, try turning it into a question. *How does the moon affect sleep cycles in some people? Why do people enjoy going to live theater? In what ways has J. K. Rowling affected children's literature? How did General George Washington's men survive their days at Valley Forge?* By writing your statement as a question, your mind will automatically attempt to answer it—and that is where the body of your research paper will come from. The thesis statement also gives your paper direction. It shows the reader (and you!) where it is going next.

Once you have your thesis question, turn it into a statement (and make sure it is a complete one). *The phases of the moon appear to affect some people's sleep cycles. Live theater presents an entirely different kind of experience from a movie theater. J. K. Rowling revolutionized children's literature in three main ways. George Washington's men barely survived their days at Valley Forge.* Can you see where each one of these statements could lead?

A strong thesis statement is your key to a strong paper. It needs vivid vocabulary. Can you see the difference between these statements?

ORDINARY	EXTRAORDINARY
Beethoven wrote some of the world's most beautiful music.	Beethoven managed to produce some of the most enduring music in history despite being completely deaf.

Which would make the more interesting paper? Which would you rather read?

What about these two? Which one packs a better punch?

ORDINARY	EXTRAORDINARY
NASA has the technology to find out more about space than ever before.	When NASA scientists created a space probe capable of hurtling through space and blasting into a comet, it became clear that they had made technological breakthroughs.

Both statements demonstrate that this research paper is going to be about the latest technology from NASA, but which one sounds more interesting?

All Research Is Not Created Equal

Step three of writing your research project—writing a thesis statement—can now be checked off. Now it's time for the step that takes more time than any other. It is the one that makes this project unique and allows you the chance to really shine.

Where Did You Find That?

It's important to remember that the sources you find may not be the best ones out there. Some Web sites, books, and articles have false information, opinions presented as fact, or outdated data that is no longer valid. It goes without saying that you do NOT want to use those kinds of resources. How do you know what is reliable to use? Ask these questions about each type of resource to help you decide.

BOOKS, MAGAZINES, AND JOURNALS

What is the copyright date? If it is more than ten years old, you might not want to use it (depending on the topic). For some science reports, you may not want anything more than one year old because of rapid developments in the field. So if you're writing about cloning, you'd better stick to the past year's publications. But if you are writing about the styles of the 1920s, a ten-year-old book will probably be okay.

Who is the author of the work? Does he have something to sell? What are her credentials? If you are looking for authoritative material on cosmetic surgery, for example, look for articles published by a plastic surgeon, not a cosmetics company.

Remember to check your library's many other resources, including its vertical or clip files, pamphlet files, inter-library loan services, periodical indices, and databases.

TIP FILE

When it comes to research, you need to make sure you use:

- a variety of resources such as books, Web sites, and newspaper, magazine, and journal articles;
- reputable resources that can be trusted;
- current resources that will not give you outdated, unreliable information.

TIP FILE

A dictionary or an encyclopedia is a good place to get some generic information for your report, but never rely on them to fill all your research needs. They are just starting points. Most teachers will require far more than these resources for your project.

WEB SITES

Who has written the material on the Web site? An author should be listed.

What was the last date the material on the site was revised? It should be noted.

Are there errors in spelling, grammar, or usage on the site? There shouldn't be.

Is the information on the site biased one way or another? Are both sides of an issue presented?

Is the site attempting to sell a service or a product?

What does the URL end in? That will give you a clue to its source. (See page 45 for a list.)

How current is the information on the site?

The endings of Web site addresses can often tell you useful information about who runs the site. Here are the most common endings and what they mean:

.com: commercial or business

.edu: college or school

.gov: government

.org: organization or group

.mil: military organization

.net: Internet administration

.sci: special knowledge news group

Digging In

Once you have your thesis statement and you know what kind of information to look up, the search can officially begin. Where can you go to find the resources you need? Here are a few of the best places to start:

- **libraries—school, public, and university**
- **Internet**
- **bookstores**
- **local experts on the subject**
- **organizations**
- **businesses**
- **museums**
- **school**

During the researching stage, your two best buddies may be the library and a computer. They have the biggest stockpile of information—and, frankly, if you aren't careful, you may soon find yourself buried under all of it. It's easy to get lost in the research process. You need to take a few precautions.

Getting lost among the library's bookshelves is a possibility if you don't know where you are going in the first place. Go to the online catalog from home or when you get to the library, and make a list of the books you want to get before you head into the stacks. Ask the reference librarian for help if you are not sure where to go. Once you find the section with the books that you want, be sure to browse and check out the other titles. There might be some that you missed in the catalog that are just perfect for your project.

Internet Research

Strangely enough, the easiest place to get lost does not even require you to get out of your chair. It's the endless maze of the Internet. You can go to one site, click on the links there, which lead you to other sites, and then suddenly, you are deep in a tunnel and can no longer see the light at all.

Search Engines

When you do a search on the Internet, don't restrict yourself to one search engine. Try a variety, including:

Google
AltaVista
Yahoo!
Lycos
CyberHound
HotBot
InfoSeek

Web Sites and Databases

You can also try the Web sites of the Library of Congress and the New York Public Library in addition to the Web sites of related government agencies, universities, and nonprofit organizations.

Check to see if your library subscribes to databases such as the National Newspaper Index, LexisNexis, and Medline. If it does, check with your librarian to see how you can access these valuable resources.

1 **When you begin searching on the Internet, several things can happen. First, you might not get many results at all.** (Getting NO results on a search engine like Google is so unlikely that people have contests to see what phrases yield those results!) If you find that is true in your search, then you might have picked a topic that is too obscure. Look back at it and make sure it is not TOO narrow.

2 **More likely what has happened is that you are not using the right terms. Check your spelling. Try another search engine. Try adding an "s" to the word and see what happens.** Also try some synonyms. If you are looking up information on fad diets, look up "popular diets," "fashion eating," "trendy nutrition," and so on. If you want info on *War of the Worlds*, you can look it up by the title, by the author **H. G. Wells**, or by subtopics such as alien invasion, science fiction authors of the past and now, movies directed by **Steven Spielberg**, or movies starring **Tom Cruise**.

3 **Of course, another possibility is that you will get 4,333,991 hits (in less than one second!) and have no idea where to begin.** If this happens, you need to **rephrase or limit your search terms**. If you are writing about the migration of sea turtles, for example, don't just put "turtles" in the search box. Even "sea turtles" will give you more than you want. Add words related to the focus of your project such as "migration" or "egg laying."

Helpful Hints for Using Search Engines

Here are a few helpful hints for using search engines:

Putting **quotation marks** around the words tells the engine to search for them as a unit:

"song lyrics"

Putting **"and"** or **"+"** between the words means the engine will look for both of the terms, but they may be separated:

song and lyrics

Putting **"or"** between the words means the engine will look for one of the terms:

song or lyrics

Putting **"not"** in the search means it will leave out the sites that include that word:

song + lyrics not violent

Is Primary Better?

When you begin looking at resources, you will come across the terms *primary* and *secondary*. Each one describes a different type of resource, but one is not better than another any more than apples are better than oranges.

Primary sources are original. You are reading the words of someone, through diaries, journals, letters, autobiographies, or interviews. When you conduct a survey or an experiment and include the results in your project, those are also primary sources.

Secondary sources are what you find in encyclopedias, textbooks, articles, biographies, and almanacs. They are written by a person or group of people who tell about something that happened to someone else or recount what another person said or did.

Is one better than another? Not really. They each have their advantages. Primary sources can be biased and emotional but authentic. Secondary sources are often more reliable but not as personal or intimate. A blending of both in your paper is best. Sometimes teachers require at least one or two primary sources and one or two secondary sources for a research project. Make sure you know the requirement—and the difference!

Info, Info Everywhere . . . But Not a Clue What to Do

Are you feeling proud of yourself yet? You should be—you have found your topic, narrowed it down, and found excellent resources. You're off to a wonderful start. Now, keep it up! It's time to take your research and organize it.

Even if you have the best memory in the world, you will not be able to remember all the quotes, statistics, stories, and facts that you read. Instead, you must take notes on what you read and you must keep them in the right order and format.

Before you read the first book or look up the first site, go out and get a package of 3-by-5 and 4-by-6 index cards. You can get individual cards or those that come in a spiral notebook. Either kind will work, but you won't have to worry about dropping or misplacing the bound cards.

The 3-by-5 cards will be for writing down the essential information about each resource. The larger ones are for taking notes on what you have learned from that source.

There are three ways to write your notes, and each one is important.

The first one is simple—write down a *direct quote* from the book. While quotes are good to use, you must make sure not to overuse them. Only use powerful, unusual, or truly intriguing ones. Don't quote statistics or facts. When you write down the quote, make sure to include every word just as it appears. Put quotation marks around it so you know that you are not using any of your own words.

The second way to take notes on your research is *paraphrasing* what you read. That means taking someone else's ideas and putting them into your own words. To make sure you aren't just repeating the original phrasing, read the material, close the book, and then do your paraphrasing. It's a good idea to go back to the book when you are done and check that your paraphrasing isn't too close to the original version.

The third way is *summarizing*. Here you take a great deal of material and condense it into a brief summary. You might be putting together information from multiple pages, chapters, or even a whole book.

No matter which of the three styles you use, you have to make sure to note where the information came from. It will be too hard to remember later when you are putting together your notes and bibliography. How you do it is up to you. Many students create some kind of code that they can remember. You might abbreviate a book or magazine title or Web site address and then add information such as page numbers or dates.

"Giving credit where credit is due is a very rewarding habit to form. Its rewards are inestimable."

—Loretta Young (1913–2000)

Let's look at a few example cards. Below is a **direct quote** from a book that I wrote a few years ago.

See the code at the bottom? It stands for page 9 of ***Violence in Our Schools*** and my last name to indicate the author. Writing down this information for each piece of information will help you know whom to credit when you use this material in your project.

Direct Quote

Violent Events Decreasing

"The good news in all of this is that although adolescent homicides skyrocketed in the mid-1980s, since the mid-1990s, they have fallen. Thanks to the ever-present media and some truly horrific incidents, this may not seem true, but Bureau of Justice statistics demonstrate that between 1992 and 1998, the rate of violent acts at schools went down from 48 per 1,000 children to 43 per 1,000. This means youth are making a turn for the better, which is a ray of hope in what was once a pretty dismal picture."

p. 9/VIOS/Orr

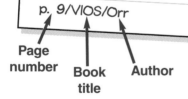

Page number **Book title** **Author**

Now let's **paraphrase** the same information.

Paraphrase

Violent Events Decreasing

During the 1990s, the number of people killed by teens dropped, although the news does not seem to show that. Statistics show deaths have decreased from 48 per 1,000 students to 43 per 1,000, which brings hope to many people.

p. 9/VIOS/Orr

See the difference? **The main ideas are there but in different words.** Now, what if you were summarizing? **You would be incorporating more material than what was in the one paragraph.** You might be summarizing the pages that surrounded it or even the entire chapter it was in. In that case, your card might read:

Summary

Main Idea: Violent Events Decreasing

School violence has been a part of history for decades. Because of the media's increased ability to cover every occurrence, it appears that they are happening more and more. Statistics, however, are showing that this is not true. Numbers are slowly dropping and this has inspired many to think that it is a problem that can eventually be erased.

p 9-25/VIOS/Orr

For every source that you are going to consult, you will need to keep cards like this. Use the larger 4-by-6 cards so you have lots of room for writing. Write one idea per card, even if you could fit more on it. Number each card so you can keep them in order. Did you notice that each example card had a title on it? This is called the **slug**, and it **states the main idea of the information**. You can scan the slugs and see which references you need when you begin putting the paper together.

While the examples given here use complete sentences, you don't always have to do that. You can paraphrase or summarize by using phrases and abbreviations. Many students use *"&"* or *"+"* for the word *and*. The abbreviation *"w/o"* can mean *without* and *"w/"* means *with*; *"@"* means *at* or *each*, and you can even use silly—but very functional—codes like *"C"* for *see*, *"B4"* for *before*, and *"UNO"* for *you know*. Feel free to invent your own personal system, but write it down somewhere in case you forget what it means!

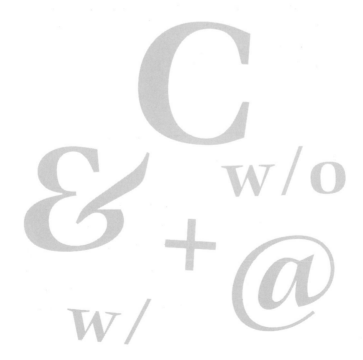

A Biblio . . . What?

The 3-by-5 cards are for writing down all the essential details you need when you put together your **bibliography** or list of sources. These cards have different requirements, depending on if you are citing a book, an article, a Web site, or another resource. Here are the pieces of information you will need:

FOR A BOOK:

You need the author, title, place of publication, publisher, and year published. It would look like this:

Jones, Jeffrey. *School Violence.* **New York: Lucent Books, 2001.**

FOR A MAGAZINE ARTICLE:

You need the author, article title, periodical title, date of the article, and page numbers. It would look like this:

Levy, Steven. "Loitering on the Dark Side," *Newsweek,* **May 3, 1999, 39.**

FOR A WEB SITE ARTICLE:

You need the name of the author, editor, or site maintainer; article title; date of electronic posting; the URL; and the date you accessed the source. It would look like this:

Scelfo, Julie. "Bad Girls Go Wild," June 13, 2005. http://www.msnbc.msn.com/id/8101517/newsweek/ (accessed November 9, 2005).

FOR AN INTERVIEW:

You need the name of the person being interviewed, the person's area of expertise, the person's address and telephone number, and the date of the interview. It would look like this:

Orr, Tamra B. Professional freelance writer. 11111 Main Street, Portland OR. 503-555-1111. July 10, 2005.

A Note on Style

Some of these note-taking methods may change slightly, depending on the style your teacher prefers. You may be instructed to use the **Modern Language Association (MLA) format**, which is commonly used for English and literature courses. Or you might be asked to use the **American Psychological Association (APA) format**, which is commonly used for the natural and social sciences. You may be required to simply use footnotes or endnotes, which are common in journalism, art, and history classes.

Staying Legal

You wear your helmet when you ride a bike. You put your seat belt on in the car. You even return your library books close to when they are due and pay the fines if they are late. So why start a life of crime now? It's easy to do if you don't take the right precautions. The crime is called **plagiarism.**

If you plagiarize, you "write facts, quotations, or opinions that you have gotten from someone else without identifying your source OR using someone else's words without putting quotation marks around them."

(*Shortcuts for the Student Writer,* Jay Silverman et al., McGraw-Hill, 2005, p. 128.) Put in plain and simple terms, plagiarism is using someone else's words or ideas and passing them off as your own.

Every time you use a fact, an example, a statistic, or a quote from one of your references, you have to note where the information came from.

(YOUR thoughts and common knowledge do not have to be noted.) To do otherwise is breaking the rules. In college, plagiarism can get you kicked out of a class or even expelled. In high school, you may get a failing grade or be suspended from class, depending on your school's policy.

Finding the information you need and getting it written down and organized is a huge part of a research project—and the most time consuming. Once you have that behind you, pat yourself on the back, head out for some ice cream, and get a good night's rest. It is finally time to take your wonderful idea, your powerful thesis statement, and your resourceful research and put it all together into a masterful research project. Let the writing begin!

PROJECT JUMP START

⭐ **Practice makes perfect.** Writing a thesis statement is so important that taking the time to practice creating them is a great idea. Write down the best thesis statement you can think of for each of these topics:

- rock opera music

- Volkswagens

- the Brontë sisters' books

- anime and manga

- cloning pets

TIP FILE

DO NOT:

- let someone else write your paper;
- claim knowledge and quotations as your own when you got them elsewhere;
- buy a term paper from a company or a peer.

BRAIN JAM:
Gathering Information

Practice, practice. Hone your paraphrasing and summarizing skills by practicing on a magazine or newspaper article. Read an article and see if you can paraphrase it when you are done. When you finish a book, see if you can summarize it in a paragraph.

May I quote you? Start listening to conversations around you. If you pay close attention, you may hear statements that would make terrific quotes.

Bookmark it. When you find a really helpful and relevant Web site for your research, bookmark it so you can come back to it later, once you're done searching for all the best places.

First draft

Mount Saint Hel

outline

Main poi

Second draft

Subpoint

THINK OUT OF THE BOX

The Writing Process Begins

MOUNT ST. HELENS OUTLINE
I. Volcano
II. Population

The Writing Process Begins

You have worked hard to lay your groundwork. Now it's time to move on to steps five and six, where your research project begins to take shape. To do it successfully, you need a writer's road map to follow and the information to create your first itinerary. In the research world, this means an outline and that important first draft.

Where Am I Going Again?

Imagine that you are going on a trip. You know you want to head west **(your idea)**, and your car is full of suitcases stuffed with everything you need from clean underwear to tasty snacks **(research)**. You have a limited amount of time **(due date)** and want to see as much as possible **(do a good job)**. What road should you take? Which one is fastest, safest, or best? **You need a road map to tell you—or in this case, an outline.**

Heading in the Right Direction

Putting together an outline is not difficult. You can do it in:

- **single words,**
- **phrases,**
- **or complete sentences**.

Some writers prefer sentences because then, when they are ready to plug their points into the paper, it feels like some of the hard work is already done. The example on page 66 is in phrases rather than sentences, just to show you how it looks. Keep in mind that your outline may change here and there as you start writing the paper. You may find that one point needs to shift up or down, or you may find some exciting new information that you just have to add. Don't worry about that. Outlines allow for detours now and then just like a good road map.

A research project, like an essay, has three main parts:

- **an introduction,**
- **a body,**
- **and a conclusion.**

But the body portion of your research paper will be extended, because this is a much longer work. Your outline should have several main points. The exact number will depend on the assigned length of the paper.

Let's say you are going to write a research project on Mount St. Helens. It may have been several years before your time, but in 1980, this volcano erupted and destroyed more than 200 square miles (518 square kilometers) of land.

To begin the outline, write your thesis statement at the top. For example:

A quarter of a century ago, Mount St. Helens blasted Washington's skies with dirt, rocks, steam, and ash, and even today, it continues to do so unexpectedly.

From here, it is time to expand on the main points and subpoints of your outline. For Mount St. Helens, it might look like this:

OUTLINE

I. **Introduction**

II. **The eruption of 1980**

    A. Effect on land and animals

    B. Effect on surrounding cities and towns

    C. Change in shape and look of mountaintop

    D. Eyewitness accounts of eruption

III. **Creation of the new lava dome**

    A. Six-year development

    B. Description of dome formation

IV. **Earthquake swarms**

    A. Interview with seismologist

    B. Map of quake sites

    C. Explanation of quake's sizes and occurrences

V. **Recent volcanic activity**

    A. October 2004 eruption

    B. March 2005 eruption

    C. Future projections

VI. **Conclusion**

SAMPLE PROJECT

Can you see how this outline gives you the map you need to write your paper in a logical order? It tells you each "place" you need to go and then where to head next.

From Outline to First Draft

Once you have your outline fleshed out, you can start turning it into your first draft. Remember that your research is there to support your thoughts and opinions—don't rely so much on it that you end up just linking a bunch of quotes with a couple of your own words in between.

Here is a rough draft of the fifth point in the outline, the section on recent volcanic activity:

FIRST DRAFT

Mount St. Helens is still quite active and rumbling. Scientists and other experts keep an eye on it at all times and a live video camera lets Internet viewers see how it is doing also.

In October 2004, the mountain erupted again. Steam and ash were thrown several thousand feet into the air and threw pieces of rocks more than a half mile. Over the next five days, the mountain continued to roar and spit, sending ash into the air as much as 60 miles (96 km) away.

Less than six months later, the mountain rumbled again. People watched as steam and smoke poured out of the top, but fortunately this eruption was too small to cause much damage.

Experts believe that Mount St. Helens will keep making noise and experiencing small earhquakes. The lava dome is growing at a remarkably quick rate and some believe that it will not be long before the mountain is as tall as it was before the 1980 explosion.

PROJECT JUMP START

★ **Try this. Now try that.** Take the following statement, complete it, and then write three outlines for it: one using full sentences, one using phrases, and one using single words. Which style do you like best? Which one do you think is most effective?

The best _____ (movie, book, TV show, etc.) in the world has to be _____.

★ **Go beyond the outline.** Now take the outline you like best and write your introductory paragraph. Did your outline provide enough information? If not, what needs to be changed?

HELPFUL RESOURCES

For more information on how to create a good outline, visit Purdue University's Online Writing Lab (OWL) at *http://owl. english.purdue.edu/handouts/general/ gl_outlin.html*

BRAIN JAM:
Fill In the Blanks

Go back to the beginning. Look at your thesis statement. Read it and see what words pop up in your mind. For example, the thesis statement we used as an example uses words such as *blasted*, *steam*, *ash*, and *unexpectedly*. If you were thinking about the topic, what words might work? What vivid vocabulary might go with a paper about volcanoes?

Start asking questions. Look at your thesis statement one more time. If you had just read that statement in a magazine article or in someone else's research paper, what questions would come to mind? Write those questions down and then check your outline to see if those answers are covered somewhere in the body of the project.

Body

Conclusion

Introduction

Title page

Stats

Fac

Intervie

Clear

Quotes

THE SPIN ROOM

Revising Your Way to Extraordinary

Revising Your Way to Extraordinary

You are coming to the end of your long list of steps. Congratulate yourself on making it through finding the topic, narrowing it down, writing the thesis statement, doing the research, organizing the outline, and penning that first draft. Now it's time to go just a little further. Let's fine-tune your introduction and conclusion, integrate your resources, and add the necessary front and back matter. Before long, your research project will be ready to leave your hands.

I'd Like to Introduce You . . .

The first part of your paper is the introduction. This includes your thesis statement and should be written in a way that will interest people. Introductions vary in length, but one statement should say it all.

AN EXTRAORDINARY THESIS STATEMENT

"How does the mind work? To answer that question we must look at some of the work performed by the mind."
—Noam Chomsky,
Language and Mind

Let's look at the thesis statement from the paper on Mount St. Helens.

A quarter of a century ago, Mount St. Helens blasted Washington's skies with dirt, rocks, steam, and ash, and even today, it continues to do so unexpectedly.

Let's make that part of the introduction. Here is one possibility:

ORDINARY	EXTRAORDINARY
A quarter of a century ago, Mount St. Helens blasted Washington's skies with dirt, rocks, steam, and ash, and even today, it continues to do so unexpectedly. It destroyed a lot of land then, and even now the threat is not gone.	Dirt, rocks, steam, and ash blasted Washington's skies a quarter of a century ago when Mount St. Helens erupted. Hundreds of square miles were devastated, and layers of ash were launched onto surrounding cities. Today, lava domes continue to build and collapse, spewing more smoke and ash into the air and fascinating and frightening people in the Pacific Northwest. Helicopters circling the site let everyone know that the threat is far from over.

This does work as an introduction, but it could be improved. Let's look at another possibility and see how it is different.

Which one gets your attention and holds it? Can you see how the extraordinary introduction gives you a better idea of where the paper is going?

Bring in the Body

The body of your project is where you support the thesis statement. It is the place that you finally get to include all of that information you spent so much time gathering. Here is where you need to merge your thoughts with the facts, statistics, interviews, and quotes you have gathered and make them all fit together smoothly.

HELPFUL RESOURCES

For more tips on writing good thesis statements, visit Purdue University's Online Writing Lab (OWL) at *http://owl.english. purdue.edu/owl/resource/545/01/*

TIP FILE

Your introduction should:

• contain your thesis statement;

• show your organization;

• let the reader know where you are going.

Go with the Flow

Let's look at an example from the Mount St. Helens paper. Here the paragraph **merges the writer's words with the words of an expert who was interviewed for the project.** Look at the difference between how the two examples combine the information.

ORDINARY	EXTRAORDINARY
Mount St. Helens is just another mountain off in the distance when viewed from Portland. It looks harmless, but it isn't. That is what Jim Sternon says. "This mountain is always shuddering and shaking, even if you can't see it. It is one very busy place," he said.	Mount St. Helens is just another stubby, snow-covered mountain off in the distance when viewed from Portland. It looks harmless, but it isn't. "This mountain is always shuddering and shaking, even if you can't see it," explains seismologist Jim Sternon. He saw the original eruption in 1980 and has been fascinated ever since. "It is one very busy place," he adds with a grin.

Can you spot the differences between the two? There is more description of the mountain in the second example. The words spoken by Mr. Sternon are introduced in such a way that you understand why he is being quoted. Not only is he a seismologist but he was there when the volcano originally erupted. Also, more active verbs are used in the second. The first uses "said," while the second uses "explains" and "adds with a grin." The quotes flow smoothly into the text instead of interrupting it.

HOW TO ENLIVEN YOUR WRITING

Integrating quotes and other references into your paper can sometimes be challenging. You don't want to keep saying "he said" and "she said." Here is a list of words you can use that will bring more excitement to your project and keep you from getting stuck in a rut.

adds	admits	asks
asserts	comments	concludes
confirms	disagrees	explains
implies	insists	notes
points out	replies	responds
says	states	suggests

Blended, Not Chopped

Let's look at another example. This time, facts from several different sources are combined. Try to pick out the differences between the two:

ORDINARY	EXTRAORDINARY
The first recorded eruption of the mountain occurred in 1831. It has erupted five times since then. The one in 1980 was devastating. There have been several mini-eruptions since then. One was as recent as March 2005. There was a tremor, and a bunch of smoke emerged from the volcano.	Eruptions from Mount St. Helens have been recorded since 1831. It erupted five times in the twentieth century, including the eruption of 1980 that was completely devastating. Land was destroyed and millions of dollars worth of timber was mowed down. Since then, there have been several mini-eruptions, including one that occurred as recently as March 2005. That tremor measured 2.5 on the Richter scale and sent a 36,000-foot (10,973-meter) plume of smoke into the air. The smoke carried ash that was deposited on nearby towns.

As you can see, the details in the second example are much clearer and more descriptive. In addition, the facts are blended together rather than put down in choppy, simple sentences. It makes for easier reading and a much better paper.

And in Conclusion . . .

With the introduction and the body behind you, now it is time to work on the conclusion. Remember that a conclusion does not introduce any new points, nor does it just repeat the same points that were in the body of the paper. Instead, it brings everything together and wraps it up. It is there to provide closure.

TIP FILE

Never introduce your conclusion with something weak like "And in conclusion, let me say . . ." or end with something trite like "And after all, who really knows?"

Something to Think About

Let's look at an example.

ORDINARY	EXTRAORDINARY
There is not another eruption predicted anytime soon. It has erupted ever since 1831. The one in 1980 was huge. It keeps rumbling, so who knows?	There are no eruptions predicted any time soon for Mount St. Helens, but with its history, there are no guarantees. As it continues to rumble and tremble, residents and scientists say they will keep checking the Washington sky for signs of trouble.

The first one just repeats some key points and does not seem to bring any closure to the paper. As Chris Van Allsburg, a well-known children's author, says, "There must be something to think about at the end."

Time to Rewind
So You Can Revise

You have perfected the introduction, merged your research into the middle, and crafted the conclusion. Now it's time to walk away, watch a movie, hang with friends, or read a book. Give yourself a little distance from the project. In a day or so (depending on how close you are to your deadline), come back to it and start revising. During this process, you will:

- **fix any grammar, punctuation, and spelling errors;**
- **check verb tense consistency;**
- **make sure you used plenty of sentence variety;**
- **insert any necessary documentation;**
- **work on transitions between your paragraphs;**
- **give the project a title;**
- **put together your bibliography;**
- **create any front or back matter that is required.**

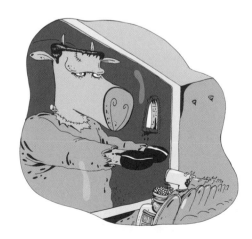

Polish Your Writing

Here's a first draft of part two of our outline (The eruption of 1980):

FIRST DRAFT

The eruption in May 1980 was really huge. It happened at 8:32 in the morning. Rock and ash flew out of the mountian top. The power in the explosion crated a big landslide.

Tons of teres were cut down and burned in seconds. Even trees six milles away were destroyed. All plants were wiped out. Deer, elk, black bears, and mountian goats were all killed and so were 57 people. Fish birds and insects too.

Houses were picked up by the landslide. So wee cars and trucks. Twenty-seven bridges were knocked down. Ash rained down in many nearby cities. It covered everything. Later it spread out and traveled a long ways.

Now let's go back and revise that piece of writing. It contains a number of mistakes in spelling, punctuation, word usage, and sentence structure. More detail would certainly make the paper stronger, too. Let's see how we can make it better by correcting each of these problems.

Note to Self:
Need to fix spelling and other errors.
Also, more detail would make the paper stronger.

REVISED DRAFT

SAMPLE PROJECT

new fact helps describe the severity of the eruption

stronger verb

The eruption of Mount St. Helens in May 1980 was **devastating**. It measured **5.1 on the Richter scale**. At 8:32 a.m., the mountain let out a **plume** of ash and smoke that rose more than **90,000 feet (27 km)** in the sky, startling passengers on airplanes. Rock and ash flew out of the mountaintop at speeds of more than **500 miles (805 km) per hour**. Minutes later, **the largest landslide in world history** lifted **1,300 feet (396 m)** off the top of the mountain and sent it plummeting down the mountain's sides.

more descriptive

new fact

specific numbers paint a stronger picture

adds impact

new fact

more specific than "tons of trees"

Within a **6-mile (9.7-km) radius**, **thousands** of trees were burned or **toppled** in seconds. All plant life was destroyed and animals were trapped. Experts estimate that **5,000** deer, **1,500** elk, **200** black bears, and **15** mountain goats were killed in the explosion. Fish, birds, and insects were also killed.

stronger verb

specific numbers paint a clearer picture of the impact

Fifty-seven people lost their lives on the mountain. Many more were in danger as the landslide **raced down the mountain** at more than **100 miles (161 km) per hour**. Houses were **ripped from their foundations**, cars and trucks **tumbled off of roads**, and twenty-seven bridges were toppled. Ash came down from the sky **like gray rain**, covering homes and cars. **Ash that stayed in the air spread out and, by the beginning of June, scientists said it had circled the globe.**

descriptive language paints a picture

new fact

specific information lets reader know exactly how far the ash spread

these phrases help describe the horror of the landslide

simile

Do you think that this revised draft is better? What did the writer do to improve on the rough draft?

Putting On Those Final Touches

You are down to the last two steps in this whole project. Can you believe it? It's time to take care of the front and back matter and then submit it.

When your teacher originally gave you your assignment, you were probably given a list of the extra materials you need to include. The most common ones are a bibliography, a notes page, and a title page. Check to see which ones are required and be sure to include them.

TIP FILE

If you have time, have someone else go over your project before you turn it in. They will see it with fresh and unbiased eyes and can more easily spot confusing places or mistakes.

A **bibliography** is a listing of the works you cited or referred to in your research project. You get this information from those 3-by-5 cards you wrote out when you were doing your research. If you wrote them down correctly on the cards, then you can simply transfer the information to your bibliography page. Remember to list them in alphabetical order by the author's last name and use inverse or hanging indentation, meaning you indent every line but the first one. It would look like this:

BIBLIOGRAPHY

SAMPLE PROJECT

Adams, G. R., and P. R. Adams. "Mount Saint Helens's Ashfall: Evidence for a Disaster Stress Reaction." *American Psychologist 39* (March 1984): 252-60.

Carson, Rob. *Mount St. Helens: The Eruption and Recovery of a Volcano.* Seattle: Sasquatch Books, 1990.

Dale, Virginia H., Charles M. Crisafulli, and Frederick J. Swanson, eds. *Ecological Responses to the 1980 Eruption of Mount St. Helens.* New York: Springer, 2005.

Parchman, Frank. *Echoes of Fury: The 1980 Eruption of Mount St. Helens and Its Aftermath.* Kenmore, Wash.: Epicenter Press Inc., 2005.

A **notes page** is where you put your endnotes, or the listing of each reference you used, as you used it. If your teacher directed you to put numbers in parentheses after each quote, paraphrase, or summary, this is where you would list the source for each of those in the order they occurred.

Your teacher may prefer that you use footnotes. Footnotes place the source information at the bottom of the page where the quoted (or paraphrased or summarized) information appears. Here is how you would indicate that there is an endnote or footnote for a fact you used:

SAMPLE TEXT ANNOTATION

The eruption of Mount St. Helens destroyed less than 0.7 percent of the forested land in Washington.[1]

An endnotes page with an entry for this fact would look like this:

SAMPLE ENDNOTE

Notes
1. Rob Carson, *Mount St. Helens: The Eruption and Recovery of a Volcano* (Seattle: Sasquatch Books, 1990), 12.

A footnote for this fact would appear at the bottom of the page where the fact appeared and would look like this:

SAMPLE FOOTNOTE

[1]Rob Carson, *Mount St. Helens: The Eruption and Recovery of a Volcano* (Seattle: Sasquatch Books, 1990), 12.

A **title page** is where you list the title of your project, your name, the name of the class you are writing it for, your teacher's name, and the date. Usually, this is all done in large font (14–18 point), centered on the page, and put in bold. Again, check with your teacher and the project directions to see exactly what is required. Here is a sample:

TITLE PAGE

SAMPLE PROJECT

Living Mountain: The Eruption of

Mount St. Helens

Jane Student

Submitted to Ms. Nelson

Honors U.S. History

January 8, 2006

If your research project includes graphics or visuals such as photographs, maps, drawings, displays, graphs, or charts, this is the time to make sure they are complete and ready to go. Have them set up, glued, colored, captioned, and labeled—whatever needs to be done to have them ready for submission.

Take a deep breath. Run a final spell-check and then hit the delicious "print" button on your computer. Your project is finished. All you have to do is put it together and submit it. Don't your shoulders feel lighter already?

PROJECT JUMP START

★ **Going backwards.**
When it comes time to revise your research project, try reading through it backwards. Spelling and punctuation errors can be easier to spot if you aren't reading the words for meaning.

★ **Critique others.** Take out your favorite magazine and look up an article. Can you point out the introduction, the body, and the conclusion? Can you think of a way that the writer could have structured the article differently to make it better?

BRAIN JAM:
Perfecting Your Paper

Here a title, there a title. Before turning in your paper, tinker around with your title a little bit. For example, if you did a project for your history class on the church trial of Galileo, you could call it *The Church's Trial of Galileo* (borrrrrrrring!) or you could call it *An Apology Far Too Late* or *Persecuted for the Truth* or any combination of much more interesting possibilities.

Read and repeat. After you have revised your paper once, put it away and then, when you've had some hours not thinking about it, read it one more time. Did you catch something you missed before? You wouldn't be the first person to do so.

Talk it over. Talk to your mom, dad, friend, sibling, or mentor about the topic of your research project. What questions do they have about it? Did you answer all of those questions within your paper? If not, should you have? Give it some thought before turning it in.

J. R. R. Tolkien

English

William Shakesp

English

Author

Po

Researc

play

Short Story

THE ENGLISH CLASS RESEARCH PROJECT

A Term Paper by Any Other Name

A Term Paper by Any Other Name

In the majority of schools, English classes are the ones that require the most research projects. An English research project will most likely center on—no surprise here—language. It might be analyzing poetry or poets, critiquing books or authors, examining the history of words and phrases, comparing two or more novels, or looking at literary elements such as theme, plot, character, and style.

Most of what you learned in the first part of this book will guide you in how to do this kind of paper. It rarely includes visuals and is instead heavily based on the use of words. The format is clear, so let's take some time to look at selecting a topic and narrowing it down just right. From there, let's develop a strong thesis statement, introduction, and conclusion.

The Topic

If your English teacher has left the topic selection up to you, then start with everyone's favorite prewriting activity: brainstorming. What have you discussed in class that intrigued you? Was there an author or poet whom you particularly enjoyed? Do the stories of **Edgar Allan Poe** send shivers up your back? Do **Elizabeth Barrett Browning's** poems bring a tear to your eye? Perhaps the fantastical stories of **J. R. R. Tolkien** thrilled you long before director **Peter Jackson** turned them into movies, or maybe the plays of **William Shakespeare** inspired you to find the closest theater. Write down the names of writers that amuse, entertain, educate, or thrill you. Write down which of their works made an impression on you. What would you like to know more about? That is the place to start.

Let's say that you are a great fan of **Lewis Carroll**. Before you took this English class, you thought he had only written *Alice in Wonderland* and its sequel, *Through the Looking-Glass*. Now, having read his other works, you are paying more attention to the poetry embedded in these two stories. So, should you write your paper on:

- **Lewis Carroll?** If you remember what we said earlier, you know that this is way too broad a subject.

- **The poetry of Lewis Carroll?** Probably still too broad.

- **One of Lewis Carroll's poems?** That would be just about right for a brief term paper.

Let's assume you are going to write your research paper on his poem **"The Jabberwocky."**

The Thesis Statement

What is it about **"The Jabberwocky"** that intrigues you?
That is where your thesis statement should come from.
**The most noticeable thing about this classic poem is
that most of the words are made up.** In lines like
"'Twas brillig, and the slithy toves / Did gyre and gimble
in the wabe," virtually all of those words are gibberish,
not actual words at all. Here are two possible thesis
statements for this paper:

ORDINARY	EXTRAORDINARY
Lewis Carroll's poetry is sometimes hard to understand yet is still quite interesting.	The surprising thing about **Lewis Carroll's** poetry is not that it is nonsensical, but that the reader still manages to find meaning in it.

With one thesis statement, the reader is not at all clear
where the paper is going to go or what it is about. **The
second one, however, clearly indicates that the paper
will explore how readers find meaning in poetry that
is buried in nonsense.**

HIT THE BOOKS

If you are interested in reading more of the works
of Lewis Carroll, go to the library and pick up *Lewis
Carroll: The Complete, Fully Illustrated Works*
(Gramercy, 1995).

The Introduction

Now let's put together a strong introduction.

ORDINARY	EXTRAORDINARY
Lewis Carroll wrote *Alice in Wonderland.* It has a lot of crazy things in it. The surprising thing about Lewis Carroll's poetry is not that it is nonsensical, but that it is and yet the reader still manages to find meaning in it anyway.	Most children grow up hearing or reading the story of Alice's grand adventures in Wonderland. They recognize the nasty Queen of Hearts or the harried rabbit who is always running late. Few may notice, however, that Alice's inventor was also a poet. The surprising thing about **Lewis Carroll's** poetry is that it is nonsensical, and yet the reader manages to find meaning in it anyway.

Do you see the differences between the two examples? **One has far more details, smoothly incorporates the thesis statement, and shows the reader where the paper is going.**

The Conclusion

How can you bring everything to a close in a conclusion for this paper? Let's try this.

ORDINARY	EXTRAORDINARY
Everyone knows Carroll as the author of *Alice in Wonderland.* Some people also notice his poems, too. He is most loved in England, where he is from. Readers especially know "The Jabberwocky." It is in *Through the Looking-Glass.* His books and poems are full of nonsense, which makes them fun to read.	Although Carroll is best known as a children's fantasy author, his reputation as a poet is also impressive. In his famous poem "The Jabberwocky," he merges gibberish with grammatical sentences and allows his readers to understand nonsense in a logical—and amusing—way.

One conclusion just repeats some of the same information. It also introduces a completely new idea (England). The other one **supports the thesis statement and brings the paper to a close.**

PROJECT JUMP START

★ **Read a story.** Pick out a short story that you like—either one from your English textbook or a personal favorite—and read the introduction. Can you pick out the thesis statement? Study how the author wrote it. What can you learn?

★ **Watch a movie.** When it's over, sit down and write the ending as if it were the conclusion to a paper. Did the film have closure?

BRAIN JAM:
Make a List

Think about your favorite author. What would you like to know about that person? What does the author do that makes him or her stand out in your mind? Make a list and see how that could lead you to a research project topic.

Science

Invention

Scientific metho

discovery

Chart

Gra

Hypothe

chart

Research

THE SCIENCE CLASS
RESEARCH PROJECT

Head Out to the Fair

Head Out to the Fair

Science class is full of discovery and experimentation. Now and then, you will be expected to take what you have learned and turn it into an official research project. You will have to write a paper about your findings, and you will probably have to include lab reports, displays, or some kind of visuals.

The Topic

If you get the chance to choose your own topic, start with the usual questions:

- **What have you studied so far in class that has intrigued you?**

- **What do you want to know more about?**

Do some brainstorming. Flip through your textbook and look at chapter titles or scan the index.

A science project usually involves some kind of experiment. It is your job to test a hypothesis, find an answer to a question, and then show your solution in words and visuals. The official name for this process is *scientific method.* You aren't just showing what you know about something; you are showing what you learned about something new that you were curious about.

Occasionally your teacher may not want experimentation to be part of your project and will instead ask for a paper exploring the life of a well-known scientist or explaining how a famous invention or discovery was made. If this happens, brainstorming is still the place to start. Write down the inventions or scientists that you would like to know more about.

Let's imagine that you have chosen to do a paper about **motion sickness**. You were inspired not only by something you read in science class about how the human ear is integral to the process of staying balanced, but by the fact that you get really nauseous when you try to read in a car. You want to find out what causes the problem and what factors affect it.

Discovering Your Topic

Here are some exercises to get your mind working:

- Describe some kind of process and then show how certain factors can change it.

- Describe a problem and potential solutions that you discovered for it.

- Describe a natural habitat and what factors affect it and in what ways.

The Thesis Statement

Let's put together a thesis statement for this project. **Which one of these seems to capture your idea the best?**

ORDINARY	EXTRAORDINARY
I have a lot of trouble with motion sickness, and in this project, I found out some of the main causes and factors that seem to make it better or worse.	The world is spinning. Your eyes are jumping. Your stomach is heaving. Your ears are not sending the right messages to your brain and you are paying a high price. Millions of people in this country suffer from problems like these and are desperate to know what causes them and what factors influence their severity.

Which one would you prefer to read? They are both looking at causes and influencing factors, but in the first one, the paper sounds like it will only be about the writer. The second one shows that this is a problem for a lot of people, not just one student.

ONLINE RESOURCES

For lots of information on doing science fair projects and research papers, visit the Scifair.org site at *http://www.scifair.org/*.

Hypothesis vs. Thesis

One note of caution. Some science teachers want you to write what is called a *hypothesis* rather than a thesis statement. This is usually an "If . . . then . . ." statement. Your work from there will be focused on testing that hypothesis. Check with your teacher and see which way you are supposed to write this before you go too far in the wrong direction.

Here is a sample hypothesis:

If a person with an imbalance problem reads while riding in a car or on a bus, he or she will become nauseous and dizzy.

HIT THE BOOKS

If you need some help coming up with an idea for your project, head to the library and check out *Championship Science Fair Projects: 100 Sure-to-Win Experiments* by Sudipta Bardhan-Quallen (Sterling, 2004) and *More Award-Winning Science Fair Projects* by Julianne Blair Bochinski (Jossey-Bass, 2003).

The Introduction

Assuming that you are to follow the same basic pattern of research projects already outlined in this book, let's look at writing a strong introduction.

ORDINARY	EXTRAORDINARY
Millions of people in this country suffer from some sort of imbalance problem such as motion sickness and are desperate to know what causes their problem and what factors influence its severity. In this project, I will find out and then demonstrate what I have learned in a paper and a display about how the inner ear is designed.	Millions of people in this country suffer from imbalance problems, such as motion sickness, and are desperate to know what causes them and what factors influence their severity. Being aware of the function of the inner ear, as well as what behavior and actions can affect it, is essential to managing these conditions.

The first introduction made one of the biggest mistakes students make in writing a paper: It says, "Here is what I am doing and here is how I did it." It announces the information instead of simply stating it. The second introduction is the one that shows the reader why this research project is important.

The body of a science research project is where you:

- **Introduce your experiments,**

- **Tell how you carried out your experiments,**

- **Explain what you learned from the experiments.**

For the motion sickness project, you would answer these questions:

- **Which behavior affected the severity of motion sickness?**

- **How does inner ear function affect balance?**

- **What new solutions or discoveries did you find that could help people with this condition?**

This is also where you will include any graphics such as a drawing of the inner ear, a chart of how events affected motion sickness, and so on. You will also have your poster or the physical proof of any experiments you performed.

The Conclusion

In the science paper, this is where you tie things up.
You have already stated the problem and shown your
work. Let's write a conclusion:

ORDINARY	EXTRAORDINARY
I found out that motion sickness is a problem with the inner ear. Twirling in circles affects it. So does changing altitude and attempting to read while in a car. Avoiding these activities is best. There is also medication to help with the nausea.	Motion sickness occurs when activities such as twirling, changing altitude, and reading in a moving vehicle affect the function of the inner ear. Although there are medications for symptoms such as nausea, the best remedy for sufferers is simple avoidance of these activities.

Which one sounds more scientific and professional?
Which one tells you what the entire experiment showed?

**Your science research project may have elements
to it that are different from most projects.** Make sure
that you know the requirements in your class before
you start.

PROJECT JUMP START

⭐ **Check it out.** For lots of fantastic info on putting together a science research project for possible use in a science fair, go to **http://school.discovery.com/sciencefaircentral.**

⭐ **Go exploring.** If you get to choose your own topic, don't just stick with general science. Look into specialties like botany, anatomy, physiology, ecology, geology, archeology, oceanography, and meteorology. Each one is fascinating and may spark the perfect idea.

⭐ **Pump up your display.** A good display should be simple and clear. Be sure to use color. Photographs and drawings get people's attention. Use safe materials and have handouts that explain more about your project.

BRAIN JAM:
Topic Boosters

Be your own inspiration. Why not look internally for a great science project idea? If you are allergic to something, do a project on allergens. If you are afraid of the dark, look into phobias. If you love movies, study the science behind the cameras.

Look beyond the natural. Check with your teacher to see if you can go past the natural to the supernatural. Can you do a project on ESP? Ghosts? Reincarnation?

Out of the lab and into the kitchen. Don't limit yourself to thinking about the type of science done in a lab when you are searching for an idea. What kind of kitchen experiments can you find? If you need ideas, check out *How to Read a French Fry: And Other Stories of Intriguing Kitchen Science* by Russ Parsons (Houghton Mifflin, 2001).

Social Studies

History

Community

city

State

cit

Governm

Co

State

Country

THE HISTORY/SOCIAL STUDIES RESEARCH PROJECT

History Comes Alive

History Comes Alive

In history and social studies classes, the world is open to you for possible research projects. You can explore events and people. You can look at what happened in your community or on the entire planet. For these topics, you will use secondary sources such as biographies and government records and primary sources such as letters and journals.

The Topic

You've heard it before, but here it is again: start with whatever your teacher has assigned or whatever idea has grabbed your attention or made some kind of impression on you. Do some of that brainstorming again and see what comes up. Here are some questions to get you started:

- **What historical figure shocks, amuses, educates, or intrigues you?**

- **Which historical event had a huge impact on your city or town, your state, your country, or the world?**

- **What time period fascinates you?**

- **What current event begs you to learn more about it?**

- **What historical document do you need to explore to fully understand it?**

Let's imagine that your teacher asked you to pinpoint what historical figure you would most like to have lunch with. Flip through your history book for some names.

Who did something that you would like to know more about?

Who was present at an amazing moment in history that you would like to discuss?

Check to see what the boundaries are for the project.

Can you invent a fictional character?

Can you study someone who is still alive?

Historical Fiction

At Clearwater High School in Kansas, students are lining up to take American history. Why? Because they like the way history is taught. Instead of just reading about it, they are given the chance to write their own original historical fiction. Working in pairs, they choose a particular period in history and begin researching it. After a month, they write letters, stories, or journal entries. That's a new spin on research projects!

Developing a Thesis Statement

Let's imagine that you chose **Sacajawea** as the topic of your research project. She was the young Native American who accompanied Lewis and Clark on their journey through the uncharted Pacific Northwest. Let's put together a thesis statement.

ORDINARY	EXTRAORDINARY
I would like to have lunch with Sacajawea because she had some amazing adventures and I'd like to hear about them firsthand.	By the time she was a teenager, Sacajawea had been separated from her tribe, sold in a card game, served as a guide for two of the most famous explorers in world history, and given birth to a son. Her incredible life, full of amazing challenges, made lunching with her both entertaining and educational.

Again, avoid thesis statements that are simply announcements of what you are going to write about. **Don't tell it; show it.**

ONLINE RESOURCES

If you enjoy history and competition, you might want to think about entering your project in a contest. Check out the *National History Day* Web site at *http://national historyday.org/02_contest/02.html* for information on the oldest humanities project contest in the United States.

The Introduction

Here is where you will set up what you would like to get out of a discussion with Sacajawea.

ORDINARY	EXTRAORDINARY
Having lunch with Sacajawea would be fascinating because she experienced so much in her young life. I would ask her what Lewis and Clark were like. I would want to know what happened to her son, who was born on the journey. I wonder what it was like to finally be reunited with her tribe.	Having lunch with Sacajawea would be fascinating because she had so many amazing experiences as a young woman. Chatting about her insights into the personalities of Lewis and Clark, what happened to her son, and the experience of being reunited with her people would make for a lively and educational discussion.

Do you see how the second example explains what questions will be covered, rather than just listing them?

The body of your project will consist of:

- **The questions you want to ask Sacajawea,**

- **What her responses would be (based on your research).**

The body of your paper would also include any visuals that your teacher requires, such as:

- **Drawings,**

- **Maps illustrating where Lewis and Clark traveled,**

- **Copies of documents from the explorers' journals.**

The Conclusion

In wrapping up your paper, sum up your interview and what you learned from it. Let's look at an example:

ORDINARY	EXTRAORDINARY
Sacajawea was a great choice because she was really interesting. Her life was full of adventure and challenges. I am glad that I chose her.	Sacajawea was a captivating lunch companion because she spoke of her many grand adventures and horrific challenges. Her incredible life made the conversation both entertaining and educational.

Taking yourself out of the mix by stating only what you learned, instead of "I am glad," makes a much better conclusion—and overall paper.

"History is the version of past events that people have decided to agree upon."

—Napoleon Bonaparte
(1769–1821)

History and social studies classes can provide the opportunity to do many wonderful research projects. They can give you real insight into the world's **past**, what is going on in the world in the **present**, and what is possible for the **future**.

ONLINE RESOURCES

Visit the **Chicago Metro History Education Center** Web site at *http://www.uic.edu/orgs/cmhec/*. There you will find links to tools that will help you create history projects as well as some samples of outstanding projects entered in the annual Chicago Metro History Fair competition.

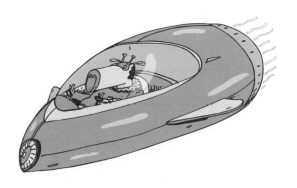

PROJECT JUMP START

I don't like you.
Instead of choosing a person (or
even an event) that you like or admire,
choose one you really do not like. How
would you have a discussion with someone you
thought was unpleasant/evil/unsuccessful/
not fun?

You are THERE! What historical event would
you like to have been present for? How would
you write a research paper that places you at
the center of this event?

Play the "what-if game." Take a historical
event and start playing "what-if." What if the
other side won? What if that person had not
died? How would either change the course
of history?

BRAIN JAM:
Fun with History

Off the paper and onto the stage. Imagine that you are writing a screenplay about an exciting historical event. Write dialogue for each of the people involved in the event.

The illustrated version. Try turning the life story of a well-known person into a graphic novel. What highlights would you include? How would you design each page?

The modern version. Get a copy of an important historical document and rewrite it in modern language. How would the document change? What words have evolved over time? What elements would you keep and what would you get rid of? Why?

TO FIND OUT MORE

Books

Elliott, Rebecca S., James Elliott, and Laurie Hamilton (illustrator). *Painless Research Projects.* Hauppage, NY: Barron's, 1998.

Gibaldi, Joseph. *MLA Handbook for Writers of Research Papers.* New York: Modern Language Association of America, 2003.

Lester, James D. *Writing Research Papers: A Complete Guide.* New York: Longman, 2004.

Levaren, Maxine. *Science Fair Projects for Dummies.* New York: Wiley, 2003.

Rozakis, Laurie E. *The Complete Idiot's Guide to Research Methods.* New York: Alpha, 2004.

Sorenson, Sharon. *Webster's New World Student Writing Handbook. 4th Ed.* New York: Macmillan, 2000.

Woods, Geraldine. *Research Papers for Dummies.* New York: Hungry Minds, 2002.

Organizations and Online Sites

Freedom of Information Act
http://www.usdoj.gov/04foia/
This U.S. Department of Justice site tells how to obtain government records.

The Internet Public Library for Teens A+ Research Writing
http://www.ipl.org/div/teen/aplus/
This site provides a step-by-step guide to researching and writing a paper and links to other online research and writing resources.

The Library of Congress Research Tools
http://www.loc.gov/rr/tools.html
This site is a great resource that describes the many different online databases and other Internet resources available to the public through the Library of Congress Web site.

The OWL at Purdue
http://owl.english.purdue.edu/
This site is an online source of help for writers of research papers and other types of writing assignments.

Science Fairs Home Page
http://www.stemnet.nf.ca/~jbarron/scifair.html
This site is a good resource for science fair topics.

The Writing Center at the University of Wisconsin-Madison
http://www.wisc.edu/writing/Handbook/PlanResearch Paper.html
This site outlines the steps involved in writing a research paper.

Need to find statistics for your project?

Here are some of the best sites to use:

American Statistical Index
http://www.fedstats.gov

Bureau of Census Reports
http://www.census.gov

FedWorld
http://www.fedworld.gov

Statistical Resources on the Web
http://www.lib.umich.edu/govdocs/statsnew

World Fact Book
http://www.bartleby.com/151

INDEX